WEARI...
GLASSES

with the
HUMAN BODY HELPERS

BY HARRIET BRUNDLE

BookLife
PUBLISHING

©2022
BookLife Publishing Ltd.
King's Lynn
Norfolk PE30 4LS

A catalogue record for
this book is available from
the British Library.

ISBN: 978-1-80155-132-8

Written by:
Harriet Brundle

Edited by:
Kirsty Holmes

Designed by:
Danielle Rippengill

All facts, statistics, web addresses and URLs in this book were verified as valid and accurate at time of
writing. No responsibility for any changes to external websites or references can be accepted by either
the author or publisher.

OPTICIAN

IMAGE CREDITS

All images are courtesy of Shutterstock.com, unless otherwise specified. With thanks to Getty Images,
Thinkstock Photo and iStockphoto. Front Cover & 1 – Beatriz Gascon J, NikaMooni, Milan M. Images used on
every spread – Beatriz Gascon J, NikaMooni, yana shypova. 2 – Visual Generation, Jane Kelly, inithings. 5 – Filip
Dokladal. 7 – kidstudio852. 8 – thailerderden10. 9 – natrot, Stock_VectorSale, mayrum. 10 – ByEmo. 11 – edel. 12
& 13 – jehsomwang. 14 – Dezay, Macrovector. 15 – svtdesign. 16 – E.Druzhinina. 18 – Iuliia Saenkova. 19 – Visual
Generation, Jane Kelly, inithings. 20 – ElkhatiebVector, Mix3r. 22 – nawamin, Katrin FTZ. 23 – Igdeeva Alena.

CONTENTS

YOUR EYES

Our eyes send messages to our brain, helping us to see the world around us. Our two eyes work together to make a 3D picture of what we are seeing, telling us information like how far away something is, or its colour.

There are lots of different parts to our eyes and they work together to help us see. Eyesight differs, so yours might be different to someone in your family or from your friends.

WHAT ARE GLASSES?

Glasses help us to see more clearly. They have lenses, which are pieces of glass or plastic that are made to help our vision. As you get older, the lenses in your glasses may change.

Hi, I'm Lucy Lens!

Each person with glasses has lenses that are exactly right to help their eyes. A pair of glasses that help one person might not make a difference for another, or could even make their vision worse.

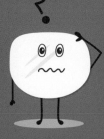

Glasses have frames to hold the lenses, arms to loop over your ears, and ear and nose pieces which make your glasses more comfortable and stop them from sliding off. Lenses can fit into whichever frames you choose.

When you have your glasses fitted, these parts will be made to fit your face perfectly. It is very important that your glasses sit correctly so that they can work their best and help you to see.

WHY MIGHT I NEED GLASSES?

You might need glasses because you are short-sighted, which is also known as myopia. If you are short-sighted, things in the distance are not clear. Road signs or the board at school might be tricky to read or look a bit blurry.

You might need glasses because you are long-sighted, which is also known as hyperopia. This means that things close-up are not clear, which can make reading and writing difficult. Other people need glasses because their eye is egg-shaped. This is called astigmatism.

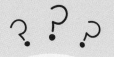

HOW DO
GLASSES WORK?

Our eyes use light to send our brain the messages it needs to see the things around us. If your vision is not clear, it is because light is hitting your eyes in the wrong place and it needs to be corrected.

MYOPIA

HYPEROPIA

ASTIGMATISM

The lenses in a pair of glasses bend the light to make it hit exactly the right part of the eye. When the light hits the correct place, it makes our vision as clear as possible. You will not be able to notice it happening, and you cannot feel it either.

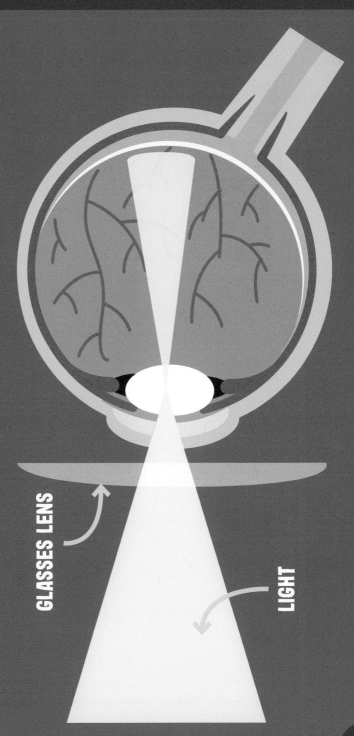

GLASSES LENS

LIGHT

WHAT HAPPENS AT THE OPTICIANS?

When you go to see the optician, they will test your eyes in different ways to check that your eyes are healthy and how well you can see. They may ask you to read out lines of letters at different sizes or shine a light in your eyes.

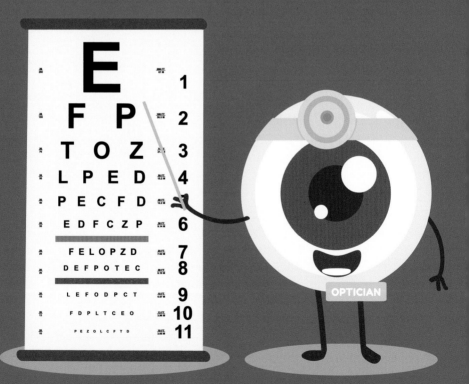

OPTICIAN

If your optician decides you need glasses, they will give you a prescription which tells you the strength your lenses need to be. Now, for the fun part! You can pick out your frames and within a few days your glasses will be ready.

WHAT TO EXPECT

When you first put your glasses on, you should notice that your vision is clearer. You should be able to see everything perfectly, especially anything that seemed blurry before you had glasses.

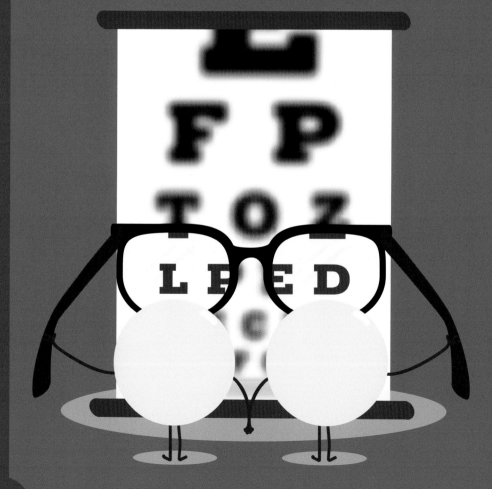

For the first few days, you might feel aware of your glasses on your face or be able to notice the frames around your eyes. After a while, you will become used to the feeling of wearing glasses.

DOS AND DON'TS

Do take good care of your glasses. Keep them in a case when you are not wearing them so that the lenses do not get scratched. Do not leave your glasses lying about where they could get damaged.

Do make sure that you go to all of your appointments with the optician so they can check that you are wearing the right prescription and your eyes are healthy. If it feels like your glasses do not fit or are not helping, tell an adult.

LIFE WITH GLASSES

Once you start wearing your glasses, you might need to take more care when playing sports. If you cannot manage without your glasses, try to be extra careful with anything that could hit your face.

You might notice that wearing glasses in the rain can be a bit of a pain. Steamy rooms can make it difficult, too. Do not panic – inside your glasses case there is usually a small cloth which can be used to clean the water and steam off your glasses.

BYE-BYE
GLASSES!

As you get older, your optician may offer you the change to try contact lenses. These are small, round lenses that go directly onto your eyeball. This means you will not need to wear glasses all the time.

You must take contact lenses out after you have worn them for the recommended amount of time. You could have contact lenses which you clean and use again or ones that you throw away each day.

QUESTIONS

1: If you are short-sighted, which of these might be harder to see?

a) Things that are red

b) Things that are nearby

c) Things that are far away in the distance

2: What does an optician do?

3: What can you keep your glasses in so that they are safe?

4: Name two things you need to be careful of when you are wearing glasses.

5: Does every person who has glasses have the same kind of lens?